"*Over the years, I have found that successful executives are rarely effective job seekers. They often lack the necessary skills, and take far too long to find their next job. Executives over 50 have the greatest challenge of all. Finally, there is a book that offers them a clearly defined process to complete their job search in the shortest time possible.*"

Ken Meyer, senior executive recruiter for Fortune 50 companies

"**Fired at 50** *provides a proven road map that executives can use to find their next job faster. After conducting a job search on my own in the most difficult job market in memory, I hired Tucker and Bob. In less than five months, using the same process and tactics they describe in* **Fired at 50,** *they guided me to land a leadership role in a highly respected firm. Their advice and counsel were superb in all respects.*"

Doron D. Grosman, Operating Partner, leading private equity firm

FIRED AT
50

How to
Overcome
the Greatest
Executive Job
Search Challenge

by TUCKER MAYS *and* BOB SLOANE

Acknowledgements

We would like to acknowledge the strong support we have received from former clients, numerous colleagues, business contacts and friends as we prepared this book. In addition, several business leaders were kind enough to review our early manuscript, and we have incorporated many of their recommendations in these pages.

Finally, recognizing the years we have enjoyed as business partners, we want to especially acknowledge our gratitude for the ongoing support and ideas we have received from Gabriella Mays and Pam Sloane, our life partners.

Tucker and Bob

About the Authors

Tucker Mays

Tucker Mays is a Principal and co-founder of OptiMarket®, LLC. He began his career in Wall Street with Goldman Sachs, and then moved to the consumer products industry to pursue his strong interest in marketing. Tucker has held senior marketing management positions with leading consumer products companies including Chesebrough Ponds and Miles Laboratories, and served as EVP/COO at global outdoor products companies Avia, Spinergy and Diamondback.

Tucker holds a BA from Dartmouth College and an MBA in Marketing/Finance from the Columbia Graduate School of Business. He is also a Mentor Program graduate of Corporate Coach University and a founding member of the Executive Forum, where he served on the board for many years and established the EF Mentoring Program.

Bob Sloane

Bob Sloane is a Principal and co-founder of OptiMarket®, LLC. He has held senior management roles with Colgate-Palmolive, American Cyanamid's Shulton International division, and the NFL. He has consulted to IBM and the White House. In 1995, Bob was the co-Founder and first Chairman of the Executive Forum, a Greenwich, CT based non-profit association of select senior executives, which is recognized as a premier executive career transition resource.

Bob holds an MBA in Marketing Management from Baruch College of CUNY and a BA in Economics from St. Francis College in New York. He has also served as Adjunct Professor, Internet Marketing at St. Francis College, where he helped lead the development of an e-commerce concentration of study as well as new distance learning initiatives.

Table of Contents

	Page
Introduction	1
I The Job Market Today for Executives Over 50	5
Chapter 1 The Over 50 Age Bias	7
Chapter 2 Overcoming the Age Bias	13
Chapter 3 Make Your Age an Asset	23
II Getting Ready	27
Chapter 4 Pre-Planning: Essential First Steps	29
III Getting Going	39
Chapter 5 Smart Time Management: Speed Your Search	41
Chapter 6 Consulting: Leverage a Part Time Role into a Full Time Job	53
Chapter 7 Executive Networking: The Power of Referrals	59
Chapter 8 Interviewing: Essentials for Executives over 50	71
IV From Getting the Offer to Accepting the Job	85
Chapter 9 When You Expect an Offer: Look Before You Leap	87
Chapter 10 The Final Agreement: Best Negotiating Tactics	95
V Advice for Currently Working Executives	105
Chapter 11 Searching For a Job While Working	107

Introduction

This book is written for you... and the thousands of other executives across America who are age fifty and older and are either out of work or concerned that they soon may lose their jobs.

Like most, you probably were or could be terminated through no fault of your own. Your company was acquired or downsized, or your boss was replaced by someone who brought in his own management team. Or, it could have been for other reasons that had little or nothing to do with your own performance. Proud of a successful career, you were confident that with a strong record and the support of business colleagues, friends, and recruiters with whom you had established solid relationships over the years, you would find a great new job in a few months.

But it hasn't happened.

After many months with no job offers, your severance has run out (if you were fortunate enough to get it), recruiters are no longer calling, and your network is drying up. You have been told many times by recruiters and companies that you have a great background but are either overqualified or "have a lot of maturity." You are surprised to find that having reached your fifties, the market considers you over the hill. For the first time in your life, you wake up worrying if you will ever get the job you want or will need to exhaust your savings to get it.

Like many other executives your age, you may never have been in an executive level job search before. You were fortunate to be promoted up through the ranks or recruited to better positions. Now in a challenging job search, you are surprised to find that traditional job search methods aren't working for you. You have given it your best, but are now in a stalled search. Confused and concerned, you don't know to whom to turn and are unsure what to do next. That is why we wrote this book.

After successful careers as leaders in diverse large, small and midsize companies, we both found ourselves in job search during the massive restructuring of the 90's. During the process, we became founding members of an executive networking group dedicated to assisting senior level executives in transition. There, we discovered that we had a lot in common, confirmed our age was being held against us, and agreed to work together to find new ways to overcome the unique job search challenges we faced in middle age. It worked, and we each found great jobs in record time.

Meanwhile, we continued to apply our learning to developing innovative mentoring programs to guide members of the executive networking group who were stalled in their job search efforts. During this time, we also gained valuable insights as to why few job seeking executives over 50 move through the process quickly, while most take considerably longer – not having a clear job objective, managing their time poorly, and lacking critical networking, interviewing and negotiating skills.

Many executives in transition asked us how we did it, and when we told them, urged us to start a business to help others like themselves. They told us that they were unaware of any outplacement firms or coaching services that knew as much as we did about how to overcome the age barrier and other special challenges executives over 50 faced. We thought about it, researched the market, and found out they were right. We decided to leave our corporate careers and start a coaching business dedicated exclusively to helping executives over 50 find their next job faster with the same new tools we had tested and used. After having successfully coached scores of executives since 1995 in a broad range of functions and industries all over the country, we decided to write this book.

Throughout this book we provide many of the tips we have given our clients, and a series of cases that illustrate how executives have successfully applied our advice and principles. These case examples are based on the experiences of executives with whom we have worked as clients as well as members of numerous networking groups with which we have been actively involved.

The purpose of our book is to explain how to overcome the age bias in the job market, and to describe the proven techniques we recommend to help you find your next job far faster than you would on your own.

I

The Job Market Today
For Executives Over 50

Chapter 1

The Over 50 Age Bias

Although they will never admit this publically, recruiters and company leaders continue to tell us that once executives reach the age of 50, firms are significantly less interested in hiring them. In this chapter we will briefly summarize the reasons why. So first, the bad news. Hang on, the good news is next to come!

1. Low Energy

After a career spanning three decades, many senior executives are exhausted by the experience, and show it when they interview. They have been beaten down by an unsuccessful search to date, lack enthusiasm in their voice and demeanor, and express little excitement about their future to recruiters and hiring authorities. Hopefully, you are not one of them. However, we have worked with countless executives in their fifties with outstanding backgrounds who have come to us for help after they had simply lost the inner strength to go it alone.

2. Negative Attitude

In many cases, executives are in transition because of a strained relationship with their boss. It could be for a dozen or more reasons, but something changed. Often, terminated executives come away from that experience with a bitter feeling about their boss, the reasons for dismissal, and how they were treated by the company when let go. For most, they had enjoyed a successful career up to that point, and never had to go through this difficult experience. Now in their 50's, they become bitter, cynical, and deeply distrustful of authority. Worse, many begin to question if they can ever work again under the intense pressure to "make it happen now!" that American companies demand. Unfortunately, their attitude works against them when interviewing with recruiters and hiring authorities for job opportunities. They are invariably turned down, and join the ranks of many others who reinforce the stereotype.

3. Lack Current Technology Skills

Too many executives have not taken the time to learn business-related computer skills including Word, Excel, and Power Point because they were provided by personal assistants or other support staff. In addition, they have limited knowledge of the Internet and emerging information technologies, and how they can be used to drive increased sales and profitability. Further, concentrating within their functional silos, they did not become skilled in, conversant with, nor did they fully grasp the power and application of the internal operating systems that are critical to improving a company's efficiency and profitability. This is knowledge that companies require their executives have today.

4. A "Corporate" Mindset

Most executives over 50 have worked for companies with extensive resources and staff support, and a structured, disciplined, and systematical way of doing business. Further, they have become used to a long decision making process requiring multiple steps and highly involved management buy-in throughout. Once a decision is finally made, they were usually able to leave most of the implementation to subordinates. This runs counter to the current demand for quick-thinking managers who can make faster decisions, and are asked to share in more of the implementation themselves.

5. Inflexible

The job market often unfairly pre-judges senior executives over 50 as set in their ways. A common concern is that they have found out what works for them as they have risen up through the ranks to positions of increasing responsibility, and are reluctant to change either their management style or approach to problem solving and people management. This is especially true for executives who have been with one company for an extended period of time.

6. Reporting to a Younger Boss

In many sectors, executives in their 40's assume senior leadership roles. Thus there is a likelihood that a job-seeking executive over 50 will be pursuing a job opportunity in a situation where they would report to someone younger. In these situations, recruiters and hiring authorities often assume that hiring an executive who is older than the person to whom they would report could be problematic. There is often a concern that there will be "ego issues," that an older executive will have difficulty reporting to someone younger.

7. Coasting to Retirement

Recruiters and company leaders worry that executives in their 50's will be less than fully committed to a new job. The risk is that they will simply do the bare minimum required to fulfill responsibilities, while primarily interested in reaching retirement. They often lack the motivation they once had in their 30's and 40's for greater responsibility, personal growth and financial reward. In addition, there is a concern that they will take fewer risks, think shorter term, and avoid healthy disagreement due to a more passive than proactive attitude.

8. High Compensation Needs

After a long and successful career, 50+ executives have been promoted to increasingly higher levels of responsibility with commensurate increases in compensation. Along the way, their lifestyle level and its parallel costs have risen substantially. Accordingly, they are often reluctant to accept lower total packages, or those that are back loaded with performance bonuses. This stance makes them less desirable than younger candidates with lower compensation needs and expectations and a greater willingness to bet on the future.

9. Physical Appearance

Far too many executives over 50 have let themselves go. They have stopped doing regular exercise and put on too much weight. This leads to an inevitable first impression that they are lazy, listless, and apathetic. Taken further, it can lead to the assumption that since they are out of shape, they lack self-esteem and self-confidence.

Summary

There are many reasons why companies are less likely to hire executives over 50 based on a series of commonly held assumptions: low energy, negative attitude, lack technical skills, "corporate" mindset, likely to be inflexible, difficulty reporting to a younger boss, "coasting to retirement," high compensation requirements, and not physically fit.

Many of these perceptions are unfair. Armed with an understanding of these challenges, you can now measure yourself against each of them and take the corrective action we recommend in the next chapter.

Chapter 2

Overcoming the Age Bias

Now the good news!

There are several things you can do to overcome the age bias. We have worked with hundreds of executives who have accomplished it. Here are our recommendations.

1. Stay Positive

Job seekers with low energy and enthusiasm often have become discouraged by rejection, and lost faith that they will ever find another job as good as their last one. For our executive clients who come to us with this mindset, we reassure each of them that regardless of how difficult and long a search can be, every executive client who has followed our proven approach has found a good job.

> *There are over 13,000,000 companies in America. You only need one, and one always needs you.*

Job search is much like finding your partner in life. Remember what it was like? So many disappointments and few successes. Wondering if you will ever find the right person. But you never stopped searching. And then one day, often when you least expected it, there he or she was. It is the same in job search. You never give up. Never stop looking. Never ask, am I good enough, or will someone ever want me. You are good enough, and there is <u>always</u> someone who is looking for someone just like you.

2. Stay in Shape

As we all know, physical exercise greatly enhances your energy. Walking, jogging, and weekend athletic activities have been proven to increase metabolism, cognitive ability, and physical appearance. Tests confirm that only twenty minutes of aerobic exercise can raise metabolism and energy to levels that can last throughout the day. Further, it is well known that exercise stimulates endorphins in the brain which induce positive feelings. It takes so little time and effort that there is no reason not to do it. You don't have to join a gym.

> *<u>Tip:</u> Get a stationary bike if you don't have one, and set it up in your home. Then find a pamphlet on isometric exercises. No need to purchase clumsy barbells. That's all you need! Every other day, take three minutes to stretch and warm up, twenty on the bike, two minutes to cool down, and five minutes of isometrics for your arms and chest. Thirty minutes from start to finish.*

Now, when the often-asked question comes up in a job interview," So what do you do for exercise?" even if you are not an avid runner, tennis player, or skier, you can answer with pride; "I have a stationary bike at home and work out regularly." Now that's an answer every potential employer wants to hear!

3. Volunteer Networking

We coach our clients to "get out of themselves" and spend time helping others. Volunteering is a proven way to strengthen your self-esteem and confidence. In a job search it is also a great way to build your network. It is advisable to do some volunteer work in a community or non-profit organization where you can meet, work with, and build new relationships among professionals who are in your target sector. This can help you demonstrate your own professional skills to individuals who can potentially refer you to new contacts in your target sector. Those who you help will often return the favor. And, it can often lead to a job.

> **_Tip:_** _Use your business skills to help inner city entrepreneurs develop business plans, put together a more effective fund raising campaign for your house of worship, library or YMCA, or serve as treasurer for a local networking group._

**Case**: David B, age 53, CFO major consumer products companies

David B. volunteered part time to help raise money for a major expansion and remodel of his town's library. During the process, he worked closely with the head of the fundraising committee who also happened to be Chairman of a large company based in the *same city – who at the time was seeking a new CFO. The chairman was so impressed by David's apparent work ethic, dedication and financial management abilities that he hired him to become his CFO.*

4. Demonstrate Your Management Flexibility

During interviews, describe how you modified your management style during your career to fit different challenges and varied business cultures. For example, you may have been working for a larger company in a junior capacity during your thirties. It was probably a "no mistakes" environment, and you were competing with many others for promotion. Accordingly, you may have been a hands-on micromanager who felt compelled to monitor your subordinates closely to make sure they always did it right. Then in your forties, in a mid level executive role with a midsize company, you discovered that you could achieve better results by delegating more of the implementation and detail so you could focus on larger, more strategic issues.

You could also describe how you modified your management style and approach as a team leader when working on special projects. This work constantly required you to adjust to changing priorities, make quick decisions with less information, produce with fewer resources, and manage individuals on an ad hoc team who did not directly report to you.

Further, demonstrate your success overcoming a variety of unanticipated problems. Examples: discuss how you responded to unexpected threats to your business such as late shipments, a product recall, loss of a major client, or new government regulation to name a few.

5. Demonstrate that You Can Work for and Support a Younger Boss

In any job interview, it is important to convince your prospective boss that by hiring you, their job and mission will be easier. This is particularly important when interviewing with a someone who is younger than you. Cite examples of your experience where because of your achievements, you enabled former superiors to succeed, to grow and advance *their* careers. During interviews, ask him what his greatest challenges in the business are, and then cite direct examples of how your skills and experience can make his own mission easier. You will be less likely to be seen as a "threat " to a younger boss if you can show that you respect his role and authority, and to convey a sense that if you are hired, you will be interested in helping him achieve his goals as well as your own.

6. Never Speak of Retirement

Many recruiters and companies will assume that at your age your primary career interest is in working for a few more years to maintain health benefits and save a few more dollars in preparation for your retirement. They will worry that you will simply go through the motions. Change their perception by demonstrating the opposite. Show your eagerness to take on new challenges, and cite the most recent examples.

> **_Tip:_** *If asked directly when you plan to retire, it is best to say that you have not really considered retirement, and feel that you have many good years ahead to continue your career.*

7. Be Flexible on Compensation

You will have a significant advantage over other job candidates when you are willing to accept less salary up front in exchange for greater performance-based bonus. Companies prefer executives who are willing to prove themselves first and "bet on the come." Decide what minimum salary you need when preparing for interviews. We have found that for executives over 50, reducing the salary requirement can often be the key factor in getting an offer; a reduction of up to 20% from your previous salary is considered reasonable.

Case: *Richard M, age 57, VP of Sales*

A former client, Richard had been a finalist twice for a VP of Sales role but was not offered either job. Two months later, he was one of three finalists for a similar position. He took our advice to lower his salary requirement by 15% in consideration of a higher, year-end sales achievement bonus. As a result, Richard became the top candidate, received and accepted an offer.

Richard's example is by no means atypical. We have counseled many executives over 50 to take this approach, and in almost every case, they obtained jobs they would not have secured without a salary concession, and ended up making more total compensation as well.

8. Describe "Intrepreneurial" Experiences

The best way to counter being perceived as "too corporate" is to cite examples in your career when you worked on special projects that required "intreprenuerial " skills.

<u>*Case:*</u> *Phil R., age 50, Controller*

Phil, a client of ours, was terminated from his position as Controller for a large financial services company. He came to us because he had been unsuccessful in his goal to become CFO of a smaller company in the same space. Phil told us he had often become one of two or three finalists only to lose out at the end. Recruiters informed him afterward that his clients liked Phil, but thought he was a bit "too corporate," and would not be able to adjust to their culture with smaller budgets and limited resources. We helped Phil identify two projects he had worked on where he successfully improved financial controls and designed a new cost accounting system. In each case, Phil led a cross-functional team that worked with a small budget and staff. Both projects came in on time and under budget. Soon thereafter, using our suggested approach, he received attractive offers from two companies. Phil had emphasized his unique combination of disciplined, large company experience and small company skills, having demonstrated a proven ability to facilitate special projects with limited resources. Phil leveraged each offer against the other, and joined a company in a role he said was the best of his life.

9. Strengthen Your Technology Skills

The rapidly changing impact of new technologies demands that executives can master the most up-to-date technology resources that apply to their particular sectors, functions, and of course their own personal communications and skills. Today's marketing managers need to know how to best apply emerging digital and database marketing techniques, including social networking, to most effectively and efficiently grow their businesses. Operations and manufacturing executives need to be aware of how new technologies and resources can improve their operations in an increasingly global competitive environment. Financial managers must know how to evaluate and implement vital long term IT investments.

An executive over 50 also needs to demonstrate strong basic computer skills, as many companies are reducing administrative overhead as individuals at all levels learn to use computer skills to maximize their personal productivity. There are several ways to easily learn basic computer skills needed for business- Word, Power Point, and Excel. Inexpensive CD tutorials facilitate learning at home on your own computer. Most states provide free classes during the day and at night. YMCA's offer classes at little cost. We live in Connecticut, and our state provides a roaming classroom bus that visits dozens of cities during the year. You can also ask your tech-savvy friends to help.

You will have the greatest leverage as a job candidate if you can convince your networking contacts as well as executive recruiters and hiring authorities that you understand and will apply the latest technologies that are relevant to your job search strategy.

Summary

There are many ways to overcome the over-50 age bias. Be honest with yourself, and when you identify one or more issues that apply to you, take the actions necessary to address them. Stay positive, keep in shape, do career-oriented volunteer work, demonstrate your management flexibility, show you can work for and support a younger boss, never talk of retirement, be flexible on compensation, identify and describe "intreprenuerial" experiences, and strengthen your technology skills.

Chapter 3

Make Your Age an Asset

Over the course of your career, you have developed special abilities that give you an advantage over less experienced, younger executives. Know what they are, and emphasize them when looking for your next job. These are beyond your functional skills in marketing, sales, finance, operations, or HR. We are referring to abilities that transcend the skills you have been taught, the talents that separate you from others. For most, these are problem solving, people management, judgment, and leadership.

Problem Solving

At age 50 or over, you may not have seen it all, but there are few challenges and problems you have not faced, or solutions you have not thought about and tried. You have learned which types of action work best for certain situations, and which do not. Having worked under pressure for most of your career, you have discovered to stay calm during times of crisis. You don't panic, or lose your composure. You find a way, because you have always found a way.

Further, since you have faced many challenges and solved so many problems, you have an advantage over younger, less experienced executives because *you can solve problems faster*. You quickly identify the key drivers affecting performance and the best solutions to shorten the time needed to improve sales and profit results.

> *Tip:* During interviews, describe examples of situations where you quickly identified and solved problems others struggled with before you such as a. delays in new product introduction b. late shipments c. cost overruns or d. quality control.

People Management

You have learned during your career that people are a company's most valuable asset. It is a given, that companies with the best people usually perform best. Knowing that, you have discovered over time how to quickly assess who should stay and who should go, and how to make those who stay even better. You will help them to strengthen their innate skills, make more informed decisions, and perform better by working more effectively with others as a team.

> *Tip:* Cite examples of people you managed who went on to successful careers, or those who struggled, but flourished when you changed their responsibilities to better match their skills.

Judgment

Good judgment is an important trait of all successful executives. Companies demand it. Your experience enables you to make better *decisions* across a broad array of alternative courses of action. From who to hire and who to fire, to where to cut and where to invest, you are in a better position to make those key decisions than younger executives because you have made more of them.

> *Tip:* *Identify examples in your recent career where you quickly identified drivers impacting underperforming sales and profits to improve results in record time.*

Leadership

When recruiters and hiring authorities are asked what executive trait they value the highest, most say leadership. As few executives are born leaders, this ability takes time to develop. Accordingly, you will probably have more proven leadership experience than those who are younger than you.

> *Tip:* *During interviews, cite examples of challenging situations where you led teams, initiated new programs and projects, spearheaded the company's shift to a new direction, or motivated your people to achieve record results.*

Importantly, leadership must be manifested in your job search as well. Leaders are decisive - they evaluate options, debate them with colleagues and trusted advisors, and know that the best way to succeed is to decide on a single course of action, and put the maximum amount of available resources to support it. As we will discuss in Chapter 4, you must develop a focused objective. If you don't have a clearly-defined job objective, recruiters and company leaders will conclude that you are indecisive. They reason that if you can't chose among several alternative paths for your own career, you will struggle making decisions on the job. Invariably, they will lose interest in you as a candidate.

Summary

As an executive over 50, if you convey your special problem solving, people management, judgment, and leadership skills and have a well-articulated job search focus, it will enable you to complete your search in the shortest time possible.

II

Getting Ready

Chapter 4

Pre-Planning: Essential First Steps

Just as you would carefully prepare for implementing any new direction in business, you should organize a clear plan before beginning a job search.

There are eight pre-planning steps we recommend for an executive over 50: 1. Organize an advisory board, 2. Create an "exit" story, 3. Write a positioning statement, 4. Update your resume, 5. Establish a personal digital profile, 6. Create a target company and contact list, 7. Develop a list of your personal contacts, and 8. Prepare for relevant consulting assignments early in your search.

1. Organize an Advisory Board

Over the years, you have established professional relationships with individuals you trust. They are people who know you and your target industries well. These can be former bosses, peer level colleagues, independent consultants, or business partners who can provide a broad perspective on how your special skills and experience best match the current landscape of present and emerging business needs. Many current or former peers or bosses have been through a senior level job search themselves, and having faced the same challenges, they can give you the benefit of firsthand experience in the process.

As the first step in planning your search, invite four to five professionals to serve as your "personal sounding board." They will provide valuable feedback with periodic advice and guidance throughout your transition. As you begin to focus your search, seek to add one or two others who would have particular insights on any new sectors you decide to target.

> *Tip:* At 50 plus, where you have been is probably not where you are going. As Marshall Goldsmith has famously said, "What got you here, won't (necessarily) get you there." Regardless of all your past achievements and experience, **it is all about where you are wanted and needed NOW.** Use your advisory board to help you identify those sectors and companies where you can best match your skills and experience to their current needs.

2. Develop an Exit Story

You will need to explain the reason(s) why you left your last job when interviewing and networking. While it may seem obvious, always describe your disengagement in a way that presents your performance in the strongest light. This will significantly influence your being considered as a serious candidate, as well as the number and quality of referrals you receive in networking.

We advise each of our clients to take the following approach when developing his exit story. First, state that your experience with the company was a positive one. Then, briefly explain why you were appointed to your last position, and how well you achieved or exceeded your objectives. Next, try to give reasons for your termination that were based on the company's situation (such as a broad restructuring), were largely beyond your control, and not a reflection of your own performance. Finally, gain agreement on the exit story from your former employer so that they will support you as a reference.

Case: *Steve R, age 50, VP of Marketing*

A client of ours, Steve, had been terminated as Vice President of Marketing for a leading consumer product company that had been recently acquired. He was replaced by the incumbent VP Marketing of the acquiring company. Steve was upset and bitter because he had always performed well and received excellent performance reviews. We persuaded Steve to let go of his feelings and move on, knowing this attitude would hinder his search.

We then developed an exit story for him emphasizing that he had (a) been hired to accelerate sales growth by creating the company's first web site, revitalizing their core business, and launching new products (b) not only accomplished this, but exceeded revenue goals three years in a row, and (c) enjoyed his experience at the company, and learned a great deal while he was there. His former boss agreed to include this powerful language when contacted as a referral for Steve.

3. Create Your Positioning Statement

In their classic book "Positioning: The Battle For Your Mind," authors Al Ries and Jack Trout created a breakthrough approach to help marketers differentiate their brands to make them stand out in an increasingly crowded marketplace. Examples: Avis- "we try harder" vs. Enterprise- "we'll pick you up." In job search, your positioning is a concise description of your search goal, and how you want the job market to think of you. It answers the question, "So tell me John, what do you want to do next?" Unlike a typical job objective that merely states the function you are interested in such as Regional Sales Manager for a durable goods manufacturing company, your positioning statement should further define you by stating key skills and what you can achieve.

Your positioning is a concise answer to the question "So Bill, what do you want to do next?" Too many fail to articulate a clear description of what they are seeking. They typically wish to "leave no stone unturned," reciting a litany of all the different jobs they could do. To a recruiter or hiring authority, this is a signal that the executive is indecisive. As we discussed in Chapter 3, decisiveness is an important indicator of personal leadership, a key management attribute sought today.

Here are the components of a concise, single sentence positioning statement which we develop for each of our executive clients:

1. Target job (title)

2. Size/type of business

3. Target sector or sectors

4. Three or four best skills

5. Business needs you will solve

Ask your Advisory Board to help identify the sectors and companies where you are most needed now. The most effective approach is to identify a positioning that combines *what you do best and like doing the most, with the kind of situations where you are most needed now.*

Here are examples of positioning statements we have developed for a number of our clients:

- *Controller for a small to midsize manufacturer needing an individual with strong financial management, treasury, audit, and governance skills to reduce operating cost and improve profitability.*

- *Vice President of Marketing, for a midsize consumer products company seeking an innovative leader with strong strategic planning, global brand building, and organizational development skills to accelerate international growth.*

- *President of a small media communications business seeking a decisive leader with strong business development, M&A, finance, and operations skills to accelerate sales and profit growth.*

- *Chief Information Officer for a mid to large size B2B or consumer business seeking a proven executive with strong communications, application integration, and business/ IT alignment skills to drive process change throughout the company.*

4. Update Your Resume

After gaining Advisory Board agreement on a positioning statement, it is time to update your resume. The resume will be more effective when it is consistent with the positioning statement you have now defined – by emphasizing those skills, experiences, and achievements that best "validate" your positioning. Top recruiters we know recommend keeping the resume to a maximum length of two pages. The greatest emphasis should be placed on what you have been doing for the last ten years, as this is of primary interest to recruiters and hiring authorities.

5. Establish Your Digital Profile – LinkedIn

Developing a professional LinkedIn Profile is essential in today's job market. It has become the largest business networking resource in the world. Accordingly, more and *more* **recruiters and companies rely on LinkedIn to find executive talent.** Many search firms have reduced the size of, or eliminated research departments as the LinkedIn database has continued to expand. In addition, increasingly more company hiring authorities are tapping into the database to find new executive talent. They find it accelerates the talent search process.

Another advantage of having a strong LinkedIn presence is that it enables you to rapidly expand your networking to new contacts. *After LinkedIn training, our clients increase their network base by 300 or more within 60 days.*

Finally, having a LinkedIn profile is an indicator that you are up to date with current technology - so important for a job-seeking executive over 50.

(Authors' note: As we go to press, it is possible that other social networking and digital technologies such as Facebook or Twitter may emerge as additional resources in executive job-seeking.)

6. Create a Target Company and Contact List

We advise our clients to use networking as the primary driver in their search. An important networking tool is a list of target contacts – individuals at significant levels of responsibility in the kinds of companies you are pursuing. We recommend a list of no more than 25 contacts. This list will change over time as you successfully reach your target contacts, and as these contacts identify new individuals you will want to meet.

By presenting a target contact list during networking, you will demonstrate that you are a professional by researching this information in advance so that you know precisely whom you are targeting, while still being open to meeting additional suggested people. *Presenting a concise target contact list makes it easier for networking contacts to help you.*

7. Develop your List of Known Contacts

Begin by developing a list of at least 50 of your best professional contacts. This group of known personal contacts is just your starting point. Most executives over 50 do not realize that it is not enough to just contact everyone you know. Importantly, your main focus is to broaden your network to a rapidly expanding group of new contacts.

Nearly 80% of all jobs are gained from someone not known when starting a job search.

So after starting with your known contacts, the key to a successful job search will be to get through the ones you know to an ever-increasing network of people you have never met before.

We'll share further insights about effective executive level job search networking in Chapter 6.

8. Prepare for Consulting Assignments Early in your Search

In today's downsizing, outsourcing market, many companies are cutting back on executive level hiring for full time jobs. Yet they still have many of the same needs for new talent and leadership. In this ongoing environment, there is far more part time and interim management hiring. For an executive over 50, this can be the perfect scenario for seeking a consulting role early in your job search. Usually the process of bringing in a consultant is a lot less time consuming than for executive hiring. It is less costly, and requires no long-term commitment.

An important advantage of consulting while job seeking is it demonstrates to the market that you have ongoing current value, and are in demand.

Approximately 40% of the time, interim roles lead to a full time job.

Job seekers over 50 make several mistakes when taking on consulting assignments while in a job search. These mistakes can delay their ability to find a good full time job in a reasonable amount of time.

> *__Tip:__ Our guidelines on consulting for executive job seekers: 1. Only do consulting work that is consistent with your positioning – so you continue to add value that is relevant to your job search strategy, 2. Spend no more than one third of your time consulting - spending more will divert from full time job search activity, and 3. Seek consulting assignments with at least a 50/50 chance in your judgment of becoming a full time job*

We will discuss more about consulting during your job search in Chapter 5.

Summary

Before you begin your job search, organize an advisory board, develop an exit story, clearly define your job positioning, organize a target contact list, update your resume and LinkedIn digital profile, list your best known contacts, and prepare to do consulting work early in your search.

III

Getting Going

Chapter 5

Smart Time Management:

Speed Your Search

Every job seeker over 50 in career transition knows that finding a job is a full time job. Eight hours a day, five days a week, and often on weekends. But few executives know how to make the best use of their time, unnecessarily delaying their search for months. They continue to use methods that are less effective now, as the job market has become far more competitive. Further, they spend too much time on what doesn't work today, and not enough time on what does. In this chapter we will advise you how to spend your job search time most effectively to find your next job faster. Since seeking a job at age fifty or over is more difficult for all the reasons cited earlier, it is imperative that you use your time wisely to avoid a protracted and costly search.

What Job Search Tactics Are Less Effective Today?

The traditional job search methods that no longer work as well in the highly competitive, "new normal" economy and job market are: relying on recruiters, published job leads, focusing only on known contacts in networking, concentrating on large companies, and seeking only full time positions. Here is why these traditional methods are no longer as effective:

1. **Recruiters**
    a. Executive recruiters now account for *less than 10%* of job opportunities.
    b. There is often a bias among recruiters whose clients usually prefer executives under 50.
    c. Engage only with "retainer" firms who will present you as a candidate to only their client companies upon your approval. On the other hand, "contingency" firms will often send resumes to numerous companies without your prior knowledge or approval.

2. **Published Job Leads**
    a. Heavy competition vs. thousands of other qualified candidates.
    b. Increasingly, skills and experience must be a *perfect match* with more demanding job specifications.
    c. Job boards continue to decline in importance as hiring companies and recruiters use the latest social networking technologies to find new talent.

3. **Known Contacts**
    a. The contacts you already know are rarely aware of a job opportunity.
    b. Most long term known contacts are usually not up to date on your latest experience and skills or current job search focus.

4. **Larger Companies- Over $ 1 Billion in Sales**

   a. Well-established succession planning, *promote from within 90% of the time.*
   b. According to recruiters, larger companies can take *9 months* **or more** to make a hiring decision.

5. **Full Time Job as a Primary Focus**

   a. There are fewer jobs, with greater competition.
   b. Full time jobs usually entail a long hiring process.

In view of the limited probability of finding a job using these traditional methods we recommend:

1. **Rely Less on Recruiters**

- Spend no more than *10%* of your time working with recruiters.

- Only contact and meet with those you know, have worked with, or to whom you have been referred.

2. **Limit Time Responding to Published Job Leads**

- Reply solely to opportunities with job specifications that are a close fit with your skills and experience.

- Allocate no more than 5% of your time in this space.

3. **Aggressively Expand Your Contact List to New Referrals**

- Approximately *75% of all jobs are gained through networking.*

- There are, on average, *four degrees of separation* between contacts you know to a referral contact who may know of an opportunity that fits your job objective. Therefore, it is imperative that you do not rely on your known contacts for job leads, and move past them as soon as possible to connect with their referrals.

4. Target Smaller Companies

- There are **20 *times as many companies in the U.S. with under $ 100 Million in sales as there are above.***

- Smaller companies are less likely to be as concerned that you are over 50 and unemployed.

- Smaller companies make faster hiring decisions.

5. Find Consulting Jobs Early During Your Search

- Hiring a consultant requires less of a commitment and avoids the cost of providing health care, social security, or severance.

- Interim and part time consulting assignments provide needed income, strengthen your resume, demonstrate your market value, and if in a new targeted sector, add an important industry credential.

Most Productive Ways To Spend Your Job Search Time

To improve the effectiveness of your search, we recommend that you allocate your time as follows:

- Recruiters – **10%**

- Published leads - **5%**
- Networking to known contacts - **5%**
- Networking to new referrals - **70%**
- Search for consulting opportunities - **10%**

Setting Job Search Performance Milestones

Now that you know how to best spend your job search time, how will you know if your search strategy is working? And what should you do if it is not? Our advice is to use milestones to assess your search effectiveness just as you would in running a business to determine progress toward goal achievement. Every month, evaluate how many job openings you have identified, and the number of candidacies, finalist spots, and offers you have achieved.

On average, executives in transition now take 14 months or more to find a new job.

Most of our clients find a new job in nine months or less. Although every job seeker's situation is different, and goals can change in varied economic climates, we advise you to set the following benchmarks to measure your search progress:

Within:	Goals
3 months	16 openings
5 months	8 candidacies
7 months	2 or more finalist spots
9 months	1 or more offers

What You Should Do If You Don't Meet Your Goals

If you have not identified at least sixteen *openings* within three months, we recommend that you add more search channels (venture capitalists, private equity firms, industry associations, turnaround companies, etc.)

If you have not been a *candidate* for eight opportunities after five months, we suggest you strengthen your resume, and improve networking effectiveness.   We will discuss best networking techniques in Chapter 7.

> *Tip:* *If after five months you have not been a candidate for a job, it is time to re-evaluate your job objective. With the help of a professional job search coaching, consider taking a small step back now in order to take a bigger step forward in the future. As examples, scale back your objective title, reduce compensation requirements, and expand geographic flexibility.*

If you have achieved many candidacies, but have not been a *finalist* after seven months, you are probably not interviewing effectively, and should engage with a coach to help you improve this critical skill.

If after nine months you have not received an *offer,* it may be time to seek input from your advisory board to help you consider different career paths such as:

- new sectors having the greatest need for your skills
- full time consulting on your own
- joining a consulting firm
- non-profits
- franchise ownership
- start your own business
- buy a business

Summary

Job search should be a full time job. In this chapter we have advised that you rely less on recruiters, published job leads, relying only on known contacts, targeting large companies, and seeking only full time positions as an exclusive focus. Instead, spend your time concentrating on networking through people you know to those you don't, targeting smaller companies, and consulting early during your search.

We have also advised that you: allocate your search time in direct proportion to the techniques that work best, set monthly goals by which you can measure progress, and adjust your search strategy based on the milestone results you achieve in terms of situations identified, candidacies, finalist level consideration, and job offers received.

On the following pages, we have provided a recommended Job Search Action Plan timeline to demonstrate how to move through the job search process using the approaches and steps we have recommended.

Job Search Action Plan

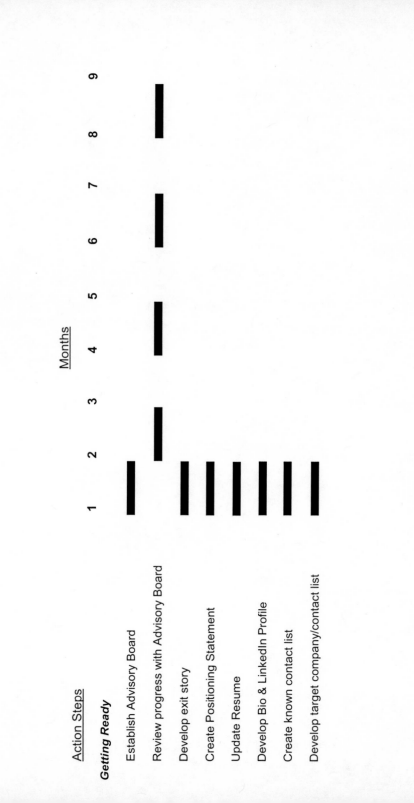

Getting Going

Network to new contacts

Send Network update e-mailings

Send recruiter e-mailings

Seek consulting assignments

Respond to published leads

Getting the Offer

Due Diligence background checks

Negotiating Final Offer

Chapter 6

Consulting:

Leverage a Part time Role into a Full Time Job

Many job-seeking executives over 50 are told, "You'd be perfect for our company, but we are not hiring at this time." Our advice is, if you are that good, but companies aren't ready to hire you full time, offer to work for them part time. Or to put it another way, if the front door is closed, try the side door.

Unfortunately, most executive job seekers today consider consulting merely as a way to bring in income after a lengthy and unsuccessful search. For the following reasons, we recommend seeking consulting assignments early during the job search process:

1. Hiring a part time or interim consulting executive costs a company less, assumes less risk, and is faster to implement.
2. Current/recent consulting achievements will strengthen your resume.
3. Earning consulting income demonstrates your value in the market.
4. A consulting role often leads to a full time appointment.

5. Consulting can be a "bridge" into a new, growing sector.

Let's consider each of these in further detail.

1. Lower Risk, Lower Cost, and Faster to Hire Part Time Executives

Hiring part time employees, especially at a senior level, is a classic strategy companies use to quickly fix pressing problems faster for less investment. Companies can avoid long-term agreements that require social security, health benefits, severance, etc. They also avoid the lengthy search process normally required to find and hire full time executives.

2. Strengthens Your Resume

You enhance your credibility and market worth by updating your career history to include consulting assignments and achievements. Including substantive consulting achievements on your resume helps answer the often-asked question, "What have you been doing since you left your last job?" It confirms that your skills and experience continue to be in demand, are highly valued, and gives you an advantage over others in transition who have no accomplishments to cite during many months out of work.

> *Tip:* *When asked why you chose to consult, the best answer is to say that the market chose you. Companies that knew of and respected your abilities approached you to help them after learning that you had left your former employer.*

3. Demonstrates Your Market Value - and Helps Pay the Bills

When you can cite current, ongoing executive consulting work, it underscores your current market value. Clearly, consulting income also helps pay the bills, especially if there has been no severance or it has run out. During a time of great stress, income reduces financial pressure, strengthens your confidence and self-esteem, and demonstrates that companies still need you and are willing to pay you what you believe you are worth.

> *Tip:* *How much to charge for consulting: Our rule of thumb is to charge* ***double your most recent annual comp*** *on a retainer basis to compensate for lack of social security (you now have to pay double), health benefits, marketing costs, and overhead/office expenses. As an example: Former annual compensation of $200K equates to $100 per hour and a consulting fee of $200 per hour or $1,600 per day.*

4. Consulting Often Leads to a Full Time Job

As cited earlier, experts in the interim management field have told us that approximately 40% of the part time consultants they represent are offered and accept full time jobs. This is because the interim or consulting executive works closely with companies, usually impresses them with his work ethic and skills, and becomes comfortable with the company's operating styles, cultures, and challenges. Accordingly, consulting can become an important part time bridge to a full time engagement.

Case: *Donna, age 53 – corporate HR executive*

With a solid corporate human resources management background at several Fortune 100 companies, Donna was terminated as a result of a corporate relocation and downsizing. She wanted to explore new sectors where there was a need for someone with her skills. Through our career evaluation process, we guided her to focus on the non-profit sector.

As Donna lacked full time work experience in this space, we advised her to seek a part time position in a non-profit organization in order to gain the relevant experience necessary to enhance her attractiveness to non-profits. We helped her find such a position, and while consulting, she expanded her networking into other local non-profit organizations. Soon thereafter, Donna accepted an offer to become Executive Director of a leading non-profit group.

5. Consulting Can Facilitate Entering a New Industry

If the job you left is in a declining industry that is consolidating and no longer hiring, you should probably transfer to one where there is a growing need for your skills and experience. Choose the one of greatest interest. Talk to executives who have successfully transferred there from your industry, and ask them how they accomplished it. As you begin to confirm that organizations in a new sector are likely to need your skills, ask one of your contacts with experience in the industry to join your Advisory Board.

Consulting provides you with a "bridge" opportunity to gain new sector experience. Once you have completed a successful assignment, you will be in a far stronger position to be hired on a full time basis with that company, or with another in the field.

Summary

Consulting early during your job search is a smart way to accelerate the process. It is a faster, less risky and lower cost way for a company to bring in needed talent. It will generate income while demonstrating your market value. Further, consulting will enhance your credibility and self-esteem, facilitate a transfer to a more appealing and/or growing industry, and in many cases, lead to a full time job.

In our next chapter, Executive Networking: Leveraging the Power of Referrals, we'll discuss how to incorporate seeking consulting opportunities into during your job search networking.

Chapter 7

Executive Networking: Leverage the Power of Referrals

Yes, you've heard it time and time again –job seeking is all about networking, as most jobs are gained this way. Unfortunately, we have found that few executive job seekers know how to conduct job search networking. *Although networking is clearly the most important tool in job search, it is also the most misunderstood and mismanaged.* Job seekers over 50 in particular make several networking mistakes.

The Most Common Networking Errors and Mistakes

The biggest error is expecting that networking involves contacting only the people you already know. Unfortunately, most of the time people you know will not have a job for you, or be aware of a current job opportunity.

> *Nearly 80% of all jobs are gained via networking to someone you did not know when you started your search.*

A second significant error entails how executives over 50 conduct a networking meeting. Over the years, we've tracked the most common mistakes executives make in asking for job networking help. From the perspective of someone who has been approached for help, the three most common mistakes reported are: (1) "The job seeker was not clear about his job search objective, expecting me to figure it out," (2) "He or she did not tell me how specifically I could be of help," and (3) "I felt that my address book was being raided."

In view of these errors, it is not surprising that so many job seekers struggle in this essential area. Most fail to get sufficient networking referrals because they fail to network properly.

Principles of Effective Networking

When advising our clients how to conduct effective networking during their job searches, we emphasize four basic principles:

1. Have a clear, concise, and well-articulated job search focus.
2. Always ask for advice and perspective on your stated search plan.
3. Never pressure a networking contact by asking if he or she knows of or has a job for you.
4. Move past the people you already know to an ever-increasing network of new contacts you have never met, because invariably that's how jobs are found.

Conducting Networking Meetings for Best Results

Here is our recommended 10-step process to help you prepare for and conduct successful networking meetings:

1. Commit to a 30-Minute Meeting

Today, everyone is time-challenged, multi-tasked, and stretched to be more productive with fewer resources in this challenging economic environment. Therefore, it is imperative that you convey *up front* to your networking contact that you only need *a half hour of his time.* Then organize yourself so you can hold true to that promise. Conduct the networking discussion as you would any business meeting. Prepare a specific meeting agenda. This disciplined approach will distinguish you from other networkers.

When demonstrating that you can accomplish your networking meeting in half an hour, you will have shown the person referring you that you will not waste the time of his valued contacts.

> *Not adhering to this disciplined approach will generate fewer referrals, and/or those referrals who are not their "A" level contacts.*

At the same time, if a networking contact should wish to spend more than 30 minutes with you, it is usually a good sign that they either want to learn more about you to help you more, or may even have an opportunity for you.

2. Start with Your Exit Story

To begin a networking meeting, first explain why you left your previous company and that you are looking for a job. Just as during a job interview (see Chapter 8), cite a reason that does not reflect negatively on your performance, but instead, relates to a change in your previous company's situation. The company may have been restructured, or chosen to go in a new direction, and your position, as well as others, was eliminated. Be brief. Spend most of the time talking about what you want to do next, not what just happened.

3. Express Your Clear Search Objective

If you are like most people, you will have a tendency to talk about numerous different jobs you could seek. It is simply human nature to want to "leave no stone unturned" and to pursue a wide range of options. For an executive over 50, there are likely to be many courses you can take going forward. Unfortunately, expressing too many options will confuse your networking contacts, making it more difficult for them to help you.

As we discussed earlier, it is best to develop a Positioning statement to express your job objective, where the key components are: title or position, type and size of business, your three or four most relevant skills, and key business needs that you can solve. See Chapter 4 for examples of various Positioning statements.

4. Never Ask For a Job

While you need to explain during networking that you are seeking a job, do not expect your contact to have, or even know of a job for you. They rarely do. Networking is best practiced when you *avoid putting pressure on a contact.* If you do not "depressurize" your networking approach, an individual contact will be far less likely to refer you to others, for fear that you will put the same amount of pressure on them. This is where most networking fails to work effectively, and as a result, job seekers are given few if any referrals to an individual's best contacts.

Instead of asking for a job, it is better to ask for advice and perspective on your job search objective, and then seek referrals to other contacts who will add further viewpoints.

Case: _David, age 54, Marketing executive_

Our client was seeking to become a VP of Marketing for a manufacturer of consumer products. We coached him to ask several probing questions during networking meetings, such as: What are the most pressing marketing needs in the consumer products industry now- product innovation, low cost alternative marketing strategies, core product revitalization? Which of my skills best relate to these needs? What subsectors in the consumer durables space have the greatest need for someone with my skills and experience today-personal care, sporting goods, small home appliance? Are there more opportunities with small, midsize, or large companies? After his initial round of twenty networking meetings, David learned that his search should focus on midsize personal care companies needing a marketing leader to ramp up revenue growth with new products and a greater emphasis on Internet marketing and national sponsorships. Four months later, through continued networking, he became VP Marketing & Product Development for an emerging company in the hair care business.

5. Cite the Consulting Path as an Option

As we discussed in Chapter 6, seek consulting assignments early in your search. During networking, express that you are open to consulting opportunities that are consistent with your job search objective. Let contacts know that you are open to interim or part time assignments, such as managing a specific project that addresses an urgent business need. You will be valued for consulting roles because of your depth of experience, which enables you to make faster contributions in solving the same kinds of problems they are facing.

6. Present a Target Contact List

Smart networkers help contacts assist them by presenting a brief list of target contacts, organized in line with the sector or sectors targeted. This does not need to be an exhaustive list, just a representative one, with perhaps no more than 25 contacts.   Note that we are referring to this as a target contact list and not a target company list. Again, you are not expecting that there will be a job at these companies. You simply wish to broaden your contacts with other relevant individuals who can help you continue to expand your perspective on the business needs in your target sectors. In using a short, representative target list, you are simply providing a "thought starter" that can prompt your contact to think of others who were not originally on his mind.

7. Lead with Your Bio, Not Your Resume

In job search communications, never lead with your resume. In addition to your age, your resume may signal you have been with too many companies, had short tenures with several firms, or shifted from industry to industry with no clear path. At the other extreme, your resume can reveal that you've only been with one company or too few companies over a long period of time.

As a job seeker over 50, your resume should not be used as a "marketing tool." Instead, develop a one page Bio that emphasizes your key achievements and company affiliations without detailing the years you spent in any one position. A Bio allows you to focus the reader on what you want them to know about you – your professional profile, key skills and talents, positions in companies where you've worked, broad descriptions of your achievements, and the degrees you have earned. This is truly a case of "less is more," allowing you to highlight the kinds of things that will set you apart for a strong first impression.

In networking, always ask your contact to send your Bio, not your resume. Then, once you have followed up and confirmed a meeting with the new contact, send your resume a day or so in advance of the meeting. Thus, the Bio has provided just enough (but not too much) information for the person to agree to meet with you. After you have confirmed that initial interest, you will have in effect been "pre-sold" to the new contact. When your resume is received directly from you just prior to a confirmed meeting, it will play a different role: providing additional helpful details about your background to "set the stage" for a personal meeting. Further, your resume information will be fresher in their mind when you meet.

8. Focus Primarily on People You Have Never Met Before

Most executive job seekers think that networking consists of contacting everyone they know until they get a job. They commonly "hit a brick wall" after all these contacts have been made, and continue reaching out to the same limited number of people over and over again. That can be very uncomfortable for the job seeker and will also put undue pressure on the networking contact.

Importantly, most jobs are found by meeting someone you did not previously know when you began your job search. In many cases, people you have never met before will be more helpful to you than those you have known for many years. One reason is that when you are meeting someone for the first time, you have full control over what impression that person will have of you – you are working with a "clean slate." In comparison, those who have known you for many years may not be as up-to-date on your latest achievements, or they may have an impression that could be out of date. For example, your longer-term contacts may have a perception of you based on a role you held years ago, from which you may have grown considerably. With people you are meeting for the first time, there is less of a "pre-conceived impression." The way you present yourself – in a concise, confident and courteous manner - will determine the way you are perceived – and the extent to which these new contacts will help you with their new referrals.

Given today's social/business networking technologies, you are no more than "four degrees of separation" from meeting someone who has or knows of a job for you.

9. Make 100 New Contacts Per Month Until You Land

Because "new contacts" are the key to how fast you will find your next job, the more new contacts you meet, the shorter the time needed to complete your search. Our "gold standard" for job seekers over 50 is that as of the third month of a job search, you need to contact 100 new individuals per month, every month, until landing. Knowing that 75% of jobs are gained via networking, our clients spend three quarters of their time using a combination of steady networking, targeted direct marketing to relevant executive recruiters, and the latest professional business networking technology such as LinkedIn, to reach this number of new contacts every month.

Case: Mary H, age 58, marketing executive

A client of ours had a successful B2B marketing career. After her position was eliminated due to a restructuring, we worked with Mary to focus her job objective, strengthen her networking skills, and use LinkedIn to enhance networking and her visibility to recruiters and hiring authorities. A few months after starting our program, Mary received a call from a corporate executive at a leading company in her city. He explained that he was seeking to hire a marketing executive, but had been unable to find suitable candidates through his HR department and an executive recruiter. He said that he had taken it upon himself to seek candidates via

LinkedIn, had found her profile, and wanted to meet. Within ten days, Mary met the corporate executive, and soon thereafter accepted his offer to join the company as Marketing Director.

10. Keep Your Network Updated Regularly

As you steadily grow your network, it is important to keep everyone up to date on how you are doing in your search. If you don't do this, many you've met may assume you have found a job *and stop looking for opportunities on your behalf.* Also, while many of your contacts may not have been aware of a good contact or situation for you at the time you met, some new opportunity may have come to their attention. Thus it is essential for you to stay "top of mind" among all contacts in your entire network. The best way to do this is to send your network a concise **update e-mail message every six to eight weeks,** to keep everyone current on the job opportunities you have identified, and your progress as a candidate. Advising networking contacts that you are in demand helps underscore your market value. And with gentle periodic reminders from you that you are still in the hunt, they will more likely think of you if a new opportunity or good new contact comes to mind.

Summary

For a job seeker over 50, networking is the most important means to find your next opportunity. Each networking session should be conducted as a focused 30 minute business meeting, during which you must be well prepared to explain your exit story, express your search objective. Always seek advice instead of asking for a job, present a target contact list to ask for referrals to others who could offer their additional perspective and advice. Understand that people you have never met before can be the most helpful. Ask that contacts send your Bio and not your resume when introducing you. Be open to consulting opportunities that support your job objective as you conduct your search. Make 100 new contacts every month until you land. Finally, use social networking technology such as LinkedIn to accelerate your networking, and increase your visibility in the market – and keep your expanding network updated regularly on your progress.

Chapter 8

Interviewing:

Essentials for Executives over 50

There have been dozens of books, hundreds of ideas, and thousands of pages advising how to conduct a successful interview. However, none have focused on the toughest interviews of all, the ones you face at age fifty or over.

Interviewing is especially challenging for executives over 50, because most are not very good at it. Why? It is simply because they have had little practice. Promoted up through the ranks, or recruited to better jobs with new companies, they never had to interview seriously for a job while not working. As a result, they haven't had to learn the keys to successful interviewing. Now in transition, facing the most difficult job search in their lives, they may be getting interviews, but not the job offers they need. You may be one of them. You know you have to interview more effectively but aren't sure how to do it. In this chapter we will advise you how.

In essence, interview is selling. In order to win, you must sell yourself more convincingly than the other executives competing for the same job. During our careers, we learned how to sell in one of the most competitive markets in the world, the global consumer packaged goods industry. From introducing new products and increasing key account sales to mass market, drug, food, and sporting goods chains to opening up new markets overseas, we learned and practiced the keys to selling success. The first thing we did when we started OptiMarket was to develop an extensive interview training program based on these proven sales principals.

The Five Keys to Interviewing Success

1. Be the Job

Successful salespeople always put themselves in the shoes of the person they are trying to sell. They assume the perspective of the prospect they are selling, and focus on that person's needs and interests, not their own. Similarly, great actors are convincing, because through practice and study, they become the very person they are playing. You must do the same in an interview. This ability is especially true for the more challenging situation when you are seeking a position that is a level above your most recent experience. For example, if you have been a successful VP of Marketing, and believe you are ready to move to the next level as a COO or CEO, conduct research for the role by studying all you can about what presidents do and how they act. Generally, presidents are good leaders, think strategically, act decisively, view and understand a company's total business from top line sales to bottom line profits, communicate clearly, facilitate group action, and inspire exceptional performance among cross-functional teams. Therefore, find examples in your career that reinforce these traits and insert them when appropriate in your interview responses. Cite the most relevant challenges you have had and the results you have achieved. Then, talk about the things you would do if you were offered the job. Describe how you would develop a new growth strategy, make decisions, and communicate with your direct reports, as well as the entire company and outside stakeholders. Discuss how you would gain buy-in from your colleagues, and motivate cross-functional teams to achieve better results.

> ___Tip:___ *Confident that you can be a president, carry yourself as if you are one during the interview. Act the part, be presidential. Dress the way a president would dress, and speak in a president's voice by talking with self-assurance and conviction.*

If you are seeking a more senior level role than you have held in the past, use the same techniques: determine the key characteristics of the position, select examples in your experience that match them, cite relevant problems you have faced and solved, and then talk about what you would do if hired.

2. Develop Good Chemistry

People prefer to work with people they like. No matter how close a fit you are with job specifications, or how well you have responded to interview questions, you will rarely be hired unless you have established solid rapport with the hiring authority. How do you do it? First, learn everything you can about your interviewer in advance. Network to individuals who know the person. College or business school classmates, former colleagues, mutual friends. Find out if the interviewer is formal or informal, warm or cold, stiff or relaxed, talkative or tight-mouthed, outgoing or shy. Is he or she interested in sports, travel, or the arts? Where did he or she attend college or graduate school?

Most interviewers will have decided within the first minute if they think you are a serious candidate or not.

It is imperative that you begin establishing rapport early on. You might begin with referencing information about the interviewer that you uncovered in advance of the meeting. For example, "I noticed that you attended Brown. My brother went to Brown, and really enjoyed it." Or, "I understand you lived in San Francisco when you were Vice President of XYZ Corporation. My wife and I lived in Sausalito when I was Marketing Director of Newco. We really enjoyed the Bay area."

If you are meeting in the interviewer's office, as you enter it is helpful to "steal with your eyes." Look for diplomas, travel pictures, works of art, and children in athletic uniforms. You might say, "I noticed you have been to Pisa. My wife and I were there two years ago. Italy is our favorite country to visit." Or, "I see your son is a soccer player. My boy just started, and loves it."

> *Tip*: *Notice if the desk is neat or cluttered. Is the room sparsely decorated or richly appointed. Smart salespeople are chameleons on a call. They adjust their style and personality to better relate and connect. Example: If the interviewer's desk is neat and well organized and/or the office is a bit sterile, make your answers short and to the point, maintain a fairly serious demeanor, and keep it "all business."*

At 50 or older, you have had a fuller life than your younger job-seeking competitors and, therefore, have a greater chance to find an affinity with the interviewer. Take advantage of the connection(s) you have uncovered and reference them in a natural, unforced way to create a bond. Remember, the better the chemistry, the greater your chance of getting hired.

3. Preempt the Age Objection

You know going in that the elephant in the room is your age. It will be the biggest hurdle you have to overcome. What should you do? Sweep it under the rug and hope it doesn't come up, or wait until it is raised in some fashion and address it then? Neither. All good salespeople know that the most effective way to counter an anticipated objection is to address it first. If you don't, the other party will probably ignore most of what you are saying because it will be less important in their mind. Your well-rehearsed responses will fall on deaf ears.

We do not recommend that you address the age issue head on, but introduce examples in your career history that reinforce your "agelessness." Refer to the age advantages we discussed in Chapter Two, and bring them up during the interview. For instance, realizing that your motivation level may be in question, talk about recent situations where you pushed for and were given additional responsibilities, or you enthusiastically took on challenges others avoided. To counter the concern that you might lack enough energy for the demands of the job, mention how much you enjoy your weekend tennis game, skiing with kids, regular walks with your wife, or morning workout sessions. If there is likelihood that your prospective boss will be younger than you, cite examples of how in your previous role you respected younger bosses, and enjoyed providing the benefits of your experience to help each of them succeed and grow.

Finally, demonstrate that you understand and have used the latest technology that is relevant to the position and the business.

The lesson here is that, right or wrong, you must acknowledge that *your age will be a major issue in interviews.* Realize that the best way to diminish its importance is to address it yourself early on with examples that convey that your age and experience will be a positive asset, and not a hindrance to your doing the job.

4. Sell the Need

One of the biggest mistakes executives make when they are fifty or over when interviewing is to lean heavily on their resume, expecting that past jobs and achievements will be more than sufficient to sell the interviewer. This is not the case. Hiring authorities are certainly interested in what you have accomplished, but are more impressed with explanations of *how your skills and experience can help them now*. You must always, always answer questions with specific examples of how your background and achievements relate to their current challenges and opportunities. Great salespeople do this. They don't talk about all the benefits their products offer, only the ones that directly relate to each buyer's special requirements.

Identify the key company needs in advance of the interview by studying the job specifications given to you by the company or a recruiter. If not available, research the company through Internet sources or reference books at your local library and via network contacts.

> *Tip:* We always advise our clients to, regardless of the question, segue your responses back to solutions that will solve their most important needs.

Hidden Needs

The most important company needs are often not found in job specifications, research reports, or articles. We call them "hidden needs." For whatever reasons, the company has chosen not to disclose them. How do you identify the hidden needs? The best way is by networking to people working at the company, former employees, or outsiders familiar with the organization. Here are some examples of hidden needs:

-CFO who is *trusted* in the financial community

-Sales Manager with strong presentation skills who can be the *face of the company* with current and prospective new customers

-*Self-effacing*, behind the scenes COO to compliment the charismatic, more outgoing CEO

-*Detail-oriented* Marketing Director to execute for a visionary CMO

Because these needs are hidden, the interviewer will usually not ask you directly to explain how you satisfy them. You have to do it yourself. Using the examples above, if interviewing for the CFO role, talk about your strong relationships with Wall Street, regulators, the media, and accounting firms. If the position is Sales Manager, speak enthusiastically about speeches/presentations you have given at company sales meetings, conventions, association seminars, or media events. If you are seeking the COO role, mention that one of the main reasons you have consistently been promoted is because you have always worked hard to help your boss do his job more effectively while drawing little attention to yourself. If you have learned that the Marketing Director position for which you are interviewing will require the selected candidate to be a great implementer, discuss how you are better at and enjoy perfecting the detailed execution of a strategy than creating one.

> *Tip:* *If there are no job specifications, and you have not been able to speak with anyone who knows the company, early in the interview, draw them out of the interviewer. Ask what personality traits he or she will value most in the new hire. What are the biggest challenges you will face? What is the company's greatest challenge? What will you need to accomplish during the first six months/ a year to be successful?*

We want to underscore that it is critical that you identify the company's most important current needs as you begin the interview to insure that you don't waste time talking about how you can help the company in areas and ways that are not relevant.

5. Ask Smart Questions

We have found that great interview questions are often just as important good answers. Why? Your questions change the reactive and somewhat "defensive" dynamic of "they ask/you answer" to a real interchange during which you seize the initiative and ask the interviewer to respond. Good questions reveal your assurance, understanding of their business, and depth of interest in the job opportunity. At 50 or over, you should have a greater grasp of the key drivers that impact a company's performance, both positively and negatively, than your younger colleagues. Use this experience to your advantage.

Importantly, the interviewer's answers will likely provide you with excellent openings to further describe how you could be of help. Note: Be careful not to ask questions that might be considered "over the line," inappropriate, or ask the interviewer to divulge information that most would consider confidential. Some examples of possible questions and answers:

Question #1

"What percentage of your current sales do new products introduced within the past five years represent?"

Answer: "About 15%. Should be higher, I know."

How You Can Help:

"At my former company, I increased the number of new products launched per year, grew the contribution of new products from 23% to 44% of sales, and shortened time to market by three months."

Question #2:

"How much of your business is overseas?"

Answer: "About 30%."

How You Can Help:

"Many companies in your sector gain up to 50% of their revenue from markets overseas. I can help you get there. For example, at XYZ Corp, I doubled our market footprint in Asia and South America, increased market share in those regions by 52%, and grew international sales from 39% to 48% of total corporate revenue."

Question #3:

"What is your approximate inventory turnover rate? How does that compare to your industry as a whole?"

Answer: "We turn it over about three times. Industry average is 5. We need to improve it."

How You Can Help:

"At Former Co. I eliminated 24% of slow-moving inventory, leading to a 16 % increase in operating margin in one year."

> ***Tip:*** *You can develop many other questions by reviewing a company's financial information (P&L, balance sheet, cash flow statements) in their annual report, Standard & Poor reports, or stock offering memorandums. For private companies, ask your business reference librarian for help researching this data from research books and Internet sources.*

Other Important Interviewing Tips

1. Limit your answers to two minutes in length.

2. Frame achievements using *the PAR approach*. Explain the problem or challenge (P), describe the action you took to solve it (A), and the result (R). Results should be quantified whenever possible. Examples: Increased sales +24%,

reduced overhead by $1.7 million, improved gross margin by 17%, saved $ 2.8 million in the first year by outsourcing.

3. Begin approximately every third answer by addressing your interviewer by name, and thanking him for the question. "Thank you, David. That's a good question. Or, "Thank you Jane, I'm glad you asked that question." This builds rapport and shows respect for the question and the interviewer.

4. At the end of every second or third question ask if you answered it properly. "Did I answer the question fully?" "Were you looking for more in my response?" "Dave, did that answer your question?" If you didn't, and didn't ask if you did, you might not get a second chance later in the interview, or worse, not be asked back for follow-up interviews to improve upon it. Further, concluding a number of your responses with a question can also help move the interview from a "they ask – you answer" format to more of an interactive, back and forth conversation, which helps strengthen rapport.

5. A personal follow-up letter or e-mail to each person you interview is of course essential. Importantly, be sure that each follow up letter makes reference to the issues and company needs you discussed in that interview, and take the opportunity to reinforce your special talents and experience that will set you apart from other candidates.

Summary

There are a myriad of suggestions on how to effectively interview. We know of none that address the special requirements of executives over the age of 50. Of all the suggestions, here are the five key techniques that we have found will consistently produce successful interview results that lead to job offers: be the job, develop good chemistry, preempt the age objection early, sell the need, and ask smart questions.

IV

From Getting the Offer to Accepting the Job

Chapter 9

When You Expect an Offer:

Look Before You Leap

In this chapter, we will discuss how to conduct extensive due diligence for a job situation as soon as you anticipate receiving an offer, and before you accept it.

Particularly during a prolonged job search, a job seeker over 50 will be relieved as soon as he or she is close to receiving a job offer. Many will be inclined to quickly accept an offer in order to get back to work. Resist this temptation, as this is the perfect time to gain additional insight about the company's culture, business performance, special challenges, and the management styles of key individuals – factors which can have a major impact on your ability to accomplish the mission of the job. You will need to collect this information quickly and efficiently, so you do not extend the process unreasonably and risk having an offer withdrawn.

Importantly, for a confidential search to replace a current executive who may not be aware that a search is underway, do not make specific reference to the particular job for which you are a candidate as you conduct your background investigation.

> *Tip*: *When you anticipate you will receive an offer, the networking contacts you have made during your search can be a valuable source of insight – either by talking to them directly, or asking them to refer you to others with knowledge of the company and its key executives.*

These are the six areas we advise our executive clients to investigate as part of their due diligence prior to accepting an offer:

1. Key Company Executives and Contacts

During the interview process, you will have met with a number of individuals. There are likely to be others whom you could now meet to further acquaint you with the company and broaden your understanding of individual management styles and the overall company culture. These could include executives who would be peer level colleagues or peers of your prospective boss. If you are considering a CEO level position, you probably met one or more Board members. Once you receive an offer, you could request an opportunity to meet one or two other Board members. Also, there may be outside executive advisors or senior level consultants whose influence could have bearing on your prospective role. Further, if you are replacing someone who is moving to another role in the company, meeting that individual is another step you may wish to take – provided the incumbent is aware that he or she is being replaced in that job.

In all cases, your objective should be to learn their perspective on prospects for the company, its current and/or anticipated business challenges, and most importantly, the key challenges you will be undertaking in your new role, as well as insights about the company's operating style: the process by which decisions are made, how internal communications are handled (meetings vs. written communications), whether staff members are encouraged to work from home as needed, flex time policies for employees, etc.

We recommend that you speak to as many of these individuals as possible to further acquaint you with the company in order for you to make a well-informed decision.

2. The Company's Customers

A good indicator of a company's condition is how it is viewed by its customers. Once a company extends an offer to you, provided there is not an incumbent in place who is not aware that he or she is being replaced, it is fair to ask to speak to a number of key customers to determine their perspective on the company's strengths and weaknesses, and its prospects for growth. Most companies will be open to this kind of a request.

It can also be instructive to speak to a company's former customers, to gain further perspective about challenges the company may have retaining customers. Identify these contacts via your network as the company will probably not identify them for you.

3. Recent Former Company Executives

In our experience, another source of insights about a company is the company's former executives. You will need to identify and reach them on your own via networking, as most companies will not want you to speak to former employees, particularly those who may not have departed on an amicable basis. Gaining the candid views of former executives can be instructive in learning about challenges, culture issues, politics, and special situations. As an example, you could gain important insights about how the company values and treats older executives.

Note: Some former executives may have left the company under negative circumstances. In these instances, consider such views with a "grain of salt." This perspective can further help you decide whether to accept the job offer, or provide early warnings should you elect to join the company.

4. Former Colleagues of Your Prospective Boss at His Prior Companies

Your prospective boss probably worked at other companies. Talking to former colleagues can provide a balanced perspective on the person's operating style – as seen by former superiors, peers and subordinates. In doing so, you can learn what it would be like to work with him. Is he or she a delegator or a micro-manager who wants to stay close to all the details? Does he or she respect the chain of command? These kinds of insights can lead you to questions you may wish to raise during a final conversation prior to accepting an offer. (See section 6 discussion below.)

5. Company Financial Information

Once you receive an offer, you will be in a stronger position to view confidential financial information that would not likely have been shared with you up to this point. Normally, you will be asked to sign a confidentiality agreement prior to be granted access to such information. Having a discussion at this time with the CFO to answer your questions would also be worthwhile.

The key aspects of a company's financial condition that you will want to view are:

- previous three-year P&L results
- three-year projected P&L plan – A concern would be a poorly explained or justified projection for sales, gross margin, and/or operating costs
- the company's current gross margin, as this will be a key determinant of the company's ability to afford business building/marketing expenditures and generate profitable growth
- three-year cash flow history and projections

> *Tip*: *Determine the company's leverage. If there is too much debt after either being acquired by a PE firm or acquiring another company, there will usually be far fewer investment dollars available to sufficiently support or grow the business.*

6. In-depth Discussions with Your Prospective New Boss

The final determinant in your decision to accept a job offer is how you feel about your prospective boss. By this time you will have had several meetings with him. Earlier, the prospective boss will have wanted to "sell" you on the job and the company, emphasizing the positive aspects of the opportunity. Also, during the process, as mentioned earlier, you will have been careful not to probe sensitive or troubling areas as it would have been inappropriate to have done so too early. Now is the time to ask these kinds of questions.

Here are the kinds of questions you should ask at this point:

- How will you prefer that we communicate? For example, how often would you like me to keep you posted on progress or any problems? Do you prefer to communicate face-to-face or in writing? What kinds of decisions would you like me to review with you prior to my proceeding?

- If not a new position, why have you decided to replace the incumbent?

- Will I have complete authority to terminate individuals on my staff? Or, are any considered "off limits" in terms of termination or reassignment elsewhere in the organization?

- Will I have final authority to hire new individuals for my organization?

- Will I have the authority to decide compensation and bonuses for my staff?

- Are there any individuals, including my peer level or above, who will be especially challenging/difficult for me to work with?

- Raise questions based on your other findings, particularly those that could impact your mission – including financial concerns, customer issues, conflicting viewpoints from other executives about the company's challenges and prospective opportunities.

- If the company is at a stage where an exit strategy is likely, what is the prospective boss's view on what that strategy could be (divestiture, merger, etc.), and how would it impact your new role?

Case: _Catherine C, 52, General Manager, manufacturing company_

Catherine had accepted an offer to join a plastics manufacturing company as General Manager of one of its divisions. She was assured by the company CEO that she would have full divisional P&L and hire and fire authority. Unfortunately, Catherine had not taken the time to investigate the CEO's background and operating style. Once on the job, she quickly learned that he was a micro-manager who questioned every budget and personnel decision. Catherine also became aware that the company had been unable to retain quality leaders of other business units because of the CEO's managing style.

After attempting to resolve the matter in a series of "heart to heart" talks with the CEO, she decided it was in her best interests to resign. Catherine then engaged with us as a client and found another general management opportunity. We coached her through the important "pre- boarding" steps to learn more about the company and the managing style of her prospective boss. Satisfied with the results of her due diligence, Catherine joined the *company and has continued successfully in this role for several years.*

7. Internet Research

Before you accept an offer, it will be important for you to conduct online research through various sources such as Google, zoominfo.com, CEOgo.com or Hoover's to identify any recent or pending legal action about the company. In the event you find anything substantial, it is advisable that you seek an opportunity to discuss this information with your prospective boss or another company officer, to help you determine if this will have any impact on your role with the company.

Summary

Once you have received an offer, it is advisable to gain extensive further insights about the company's business, culture, challenges, as well as the managing style of your prospective new boss before you accept. Having this information will give you the basis to decide whether to accept an offer. It can also provide a basis to negotiate a more attractive offer, particularly if you have learned of difficult challenges not previously known. In our next chapter, we'll discuss the best ways to conduct final negotiation of the offer.

Chapter 10

The Final Agreement:

Best Negotiating Tactics

A company has made you an offer. It may have been verbal or in writing. The initial offer probably defines your title, a brief summary of your responsibilities, to whom you report, compensation, health benefits, and vacation. They have asked you to respond. *It is imperative that any offer be in writing,* whether a detailed contract proposal or short one page agreement. Insist on it. Once received, we recommend that you thank them, and say that you would like to consider it for a couple of days and get back to them. It is usually advisable to review the offer with an attorney.

At age 50 or over, how you respond depends upon many factors including your current circumstances and the opportunity itself. You need time to sort it out. In this chapter, we will discuss eighteen important agreement criteria to evaluate. We will then provide the six rules to follow when negotiating an agreement.

To guide you through this process, let's first review the elements that should be included in most agreements and how you should address them.

Agreement Criteria

1. To whom you report

2. Your title

3. Annual base salary

   a. In addition, you may wish to ask for a signing bonus, especially if received with other companies. A signing bonus can also be used to increase your initial cash compensation if the base salary offer is less than what you are targeting, or less than your most recent salary.

4. Performance bonus

   a. Must be specific. Most are not. Need well-defined objectives linked to reward(s) paid at certain times (monthly, quarterly, annually).

   > ___Tip:___ *It is preferable that your bonus be based as closely as possible to your own performance. If it is too dependent on the company's overall results, you could end up receiving a lower bonus than expected and deserved for your own goal achievement if the company or its parent does not reach its goal.*

   b. Bonus should be equal to or greater than your most recent plan.

5. Profit sharing

   a. Consistent with your peers at the company.
   b. No less than with your former company.

6. Stock options

   a. Qualified or non-qualified.
   b. Vesting schedule. Usually three to four years; one quarter of total stock awarded after the completion of each year of service.
   c. Consult your own tax consultant if not provided by the company. Tax consequences to you can be significant.
   d. Consider asking that the first year be vested upon joining the company if a sign on bonus is not offered.

7. Length of contract

   a. Should be comparable to other company executives at your level. Ask for nothing less if you must relocate.

8. Scope of authority

   a. Often left out, but important to include.
   b. Insure that your level of authority is equal to your responsibility. You want to minimize chances of being held responsible for company actions and results beyond your power and control.

> ***Tip***: *Here is where the agreement should spell out the extent of your authority to hire and terminate, set and manage budgets, make decisions, and define expense level signatory authority.*

9. Severance

   a. For how long, when paid, and under what circumstance.

b.   At age 50 or older, *this is the most important part of your agreement.* Given the length of time it will take to get another job in the event you are terminated, bargain hard for one year of severance. If not, ask for six months. Depending on your personal circumstances/ financial situation, if offered less than six months (for example, the company offers no more than the common policy of two weeks of severance per year of service), this lack of reasonable security *could very well be a deal breaker for you.* Circumstances should be "for cause," limited to commission of a felony or breaking specified company policies such as confidentiality, or holding another outside job, etc.

c.   We believe that extended severance protection is so important for executives over 50, you should consider either giving up/or accepting less of other benefits to receive it.

10. Non-Compete

a. Bargain for as narrow a scope as possible.

b. Language should only prevent you from seeking future employment with organizations that are in exactly the same business selling precisely the same products or services. The broader the scope, the more limited your future job possibilities if terminated.

c. The length of time of a non-compete provision should be at least equal to the time period of severance provided. It is unreasonable to be prevented from seeking employment in the same type of business for a year if you are only offered six months of severance.

11. A board member role

   a. Define and limit your exposure should the company be judged liable for civil or criminal offenses
   b. Responsibilities and voting rights must be clearly spelled out.
   c. Consult an attorney to make sure you are fully protected.

12. Executive Committee membership

   a. As we advise our senior level executive clients, we recommend that you request a place on the executive committee so you will be involved in all the significant decisions impacting the company's current strategies and operations, as well as your own job.
   b. Membership enhances your credibility if you seek a job with another company.

13. Change of control

   a. Often omitted, but important. Stipulates that an acquiring company must honor your agreement in all respects.

14. Constructive termination

   a. This will give you protection should the company substantially change your job responsibilities, compensation package, work location, or reporting relationship. Having a constructive termination clause helps prevent the company from making such changes as a means of getting you to resign so that they will not be obligated by the terms of your agreement.

b. Examples: The company might require you to move to an undesirable location, downgrade your responsibilities, change your reporting relationship, or reduce your salary.

c. Best to work with an attorney to list the possible actions unacceptable to you, so that if they occur, you can claim you have been constructively terminated and are due all that is included in your agreement.

15. Benefits

    a. Consistent with company policy.

16. Relocation expenses

a. A must if you have to move and sell your house. Should be equal to those at your level in the company.

b. Check other programs granted to friends and business colleagues in similar jobs and circumstances.

17. Vacation

a. Comparable to the time provided to peer level executives

b. Seek at least as much vacation time as you were given in your last job.

18. Commuting Expenses

a. If the company is located a substantial distance from your current home, you may prefer not to relocate and instead commute. Often it will be prudent to consider a long distance "commute," delaying a full relocation commitment for you and your family until after you have become well-established in your new job.

b. Ask the company to pay for all or a significant portion of the cost for a period of at least three months.

Now that we have discussed all of the important agreement criteria, here are five rules we recommend you follow to obtain the best possible contract agreement.

The Five New Rules for a Successful Contract Negotiation

1. Try not to set a bottom line.

Most executives over 50 make a mistake in establishing a "trip wire" in advance of negotiations. For example, they have decided not to accept a salary offer below a certain level. This tactic can be self-defeating as the company may not budge, and might even withdraw the offer.

Further, you may be able to bargain for other compensation components that could be worth more to you than the higher base salary such as a larger performance bonus, more equity, or longer severance protection.

> _**Tip:**_ _If considering a lower starting base salary than your objective, you could ask for a performance review after six months so that, if you deliver specific results, this will trigger a salary increase raising you to the original figure you wanted._

Always keep your options open. When faced with a stalemate, seek alternatives for mutual gain.

2. If you must establish a bottom line, be prepared to walk
    away if it isn't offered.

In some cases, it may be in your best interest to insist on
certain agreement provisions that, if not met, would lead to
no agreement on your part. Examples might be inadequate
severance, an insufficient relocation package that is lower
than your expected costs, or a non- compete that is too
restrictive.   Base your requests on reasonable positions
recommended, such as: severance equal to others at your
level both inside and/or outside the company in the same
industry, relocation commensurate with business colleagues,
and non- compete duration that is equal to severance.

> *__Tip:__ The negotiator in the most powerful position at*
> *the table is the one who is most willing to walk*
> *away without an agreement.*

3.   Base your position on objective criteria.

The more your requests are based on credible third party
sources, the greater your chance of winning. For example,
there are web sites such as salary.com that provide salary
levels for hundreds of positions in a broad range of
industries, and cost of living indexes for many cities/metro
areas around the country. Severance, relocation, vacation,
etc. should be comparable to others at your level within the
company and no less than what you received with your
former employer.

4. Don't get personal.

Focus on the issues, not the personalities. Keep every discussion on a professional, objective level. Try to understand the interests and rationale that are the basis for their position. If you are able to determine their interests, you are better able to match yours to theirs and reach agreement.

For example, if your potential boss offers you a lower salary than you earned in your last job, ask him why. Often he will say that the company is following strict guidelines for executives at a particular level, and that to depart from those guidelines would be disruptive for the current executive staff. Or he might say that he was disappointed by the poor performance of the outside hire you are replacing, and wants to reduce his risk by investing less this time. In either case, as a response to such a rationale, you could say you understand, and are willing to take less now to reduce his risk in exchange for a near term performance review, or a larger "catch up "bonus later as you are confident you will meet his goals and expectations.

5. Treat contract negotiation as your most important interview.

This is the last and most important rule of all. Until both sides reach agreement, you do not have a job, and they do not have you. Contract negotiations usually reveal more about you, the company, and the people with whom you are negotiating than any of your previous interviews. It is a pressured situation for all, and stress can bring out both the best and worst in individuals. If either side comes across as unreasonable or unfair, or not to be bargaining in good faith, it can lead to no agreement. Always be professional, respectful, and reasonable with your requests.

Carry yourself as if you were in an interview, and use the techniques we described in Chapter 8 to enhance your position:

- Listen carefully to fully understand their positions, and the underlying reasons behind them.
- Determine their needs and try to match your skills and experience with each of them.
- Maintain good rapport throughout, and keep the discussion positive and upbeat. Always convey a sense that you want to reach a mutually agreeable conclusion.
- Prepare for possible objections to your agreement criteria and preempt them by acknowledging each one first and offer solutions for mutual gain.
- Ask questions that confirm your intelligence and understanding of the company and its interests.

Summary

After addressing the 18 essential elements in an agreement, there are five rules that an executive over 50 should follow in every contract negotiation to maximize the components of their agreement and to protect their interests: try not to set a bottom line, if you must set a bottom line be prepared to walk away if you don't achieve it, always base your positions on objective criteria, don't get personal, and treat contract negotiation as your most important interview.

V

Advice For Currently Working Executives

Chapter 11

Searching For a Job While Working

This chapter is written for the thousands of executives over 50 – or approaching that age - who are currently working but have reasons to believe that they will be let go in the near future. Perhaps you are one of them. It may be that your relationship with your boss has changed, your company has been acquired, your boss was fired and you believe his replacement will bring in his own team, or any number of other reasons. Frustrated, you have little free time to dedicate to a job search, and are concerned about keeping it confidential. You are afraid if the company finds out that you are actively seeking employment elsewhere you will be fired immediately. What should you do?

Several years ago, we experienced a substantial increase in the number of executives who wanted to engage with our firm because they were convinced the days at their companies were numbered. The demand became so great that we developed a new service, custom designed for their special needs. We call it the *Silent Partner Program*. In this chapter, we will describe several of its important elements.

There is a major advantage to seeking another job while you are working. As discussed earlier, recruiters and hiring authorities at companies have a recognized bias against executives who are in transition. You obviously do not have to overcome this obstacle if you are seeking a new job while in a job. However, you will still face the age bias plus the added challenges of finding sufficient time to conduct your search, and doing it confidentially.

Finding Time to Search

We advise our clients to spend up to a minimum of twelve hours a week in order to conduct a meaningful search. Given our time management advice in Chapter 5 this means you should spend nine hours networking, one hour communicating with recruiters, one hour responding to published job leads, and one hour working on other activities such as doing online research about key industry trends, business needs and emerging opportunities. This equates to devoting two hours each weekday and two hours on the weekend on your job search. During the business day, our working clients manage to carve out two hours during lunch, or early hours prior to the start of the business day, after hours when most personnel have left, during their commute, or when traveling. Some often find time after dinner at home.

Assuming you wish to stay in the same industry, we further advise that you discreetly network with new contacts from other companies in your space at industry conventions, conferences, or trade shows. This is an ideal venue for job search networking given the high concentration of companies present in your target arena.

If you wish to relocate to another region of the country, try to arrange a business trip to the area, and set up networking meetings there with selected recruiters and target contacts at companies of interest in advance during non-business hours.

Preserving Confidentiality

There are several ways to protect yourself while conducting a search when working. First, never tell anyone that you are looking for another job because you are dissatisfied with the one you have. If this gets back to the company, there is a good chance that you will be fired. Instead, say that you enjoy your work and the company, are always open to new opportunities, and are exploring the current job market.

Second, do not send out an e-mail blast with your resume to a database of recruiters. This indicates that you are in a serious job search. It is possible that one or more of the recruiters who have received your cover note and resume may know someone at your firm and advise them. It is advisable to reach out only to those recruiters you know well or to whom you have been referred by others you trust.

Third, there is a way to reach an expanded number of companies and recruiters without compromising confidentiality, and that is through a third party. Chose a trusted colleague, mentor, or advisor to write a personal and confidential introductory letter on your behalf that summarizes your skills and experience along with a personal endorsement. The letter would not identify you by name or company affiliation, and requests that interested parties respond to the writer. You can then respond to those of interest, explain that you have cloaked your identity because you are currently working, ask for more information about the company, and then if you think it is appropriate, divulge your personal contact information and seek a confidential meeting.

Finally, never use your company email account as it is the property of the company, is intended for its business use only, and is often monitored. Instead, set up a personal Hotmail or similar e-mail account, and/or restrict your office hour Internet search to a personal laptop or handheld PDA device.

Summary

As soon as you believe there is a strong possibility that you will be let go by your company, start planning to look for another job. You are in the strongest position to find one while you are working. Ideally, by following all the earlier recommendations in this book, and our above advice about how to create the necessary time and preserve confidentiality, you can be hired before you are terminated or soon thereafter.

OptiMarket is an executive coaching service co-founded in 2001 to provide executives with personalized two-on-one coaching and customized skills, tools and training to find their job in the shortest time possible.

You may wish to visit our web site at <u>www.optimarketllc.com</u> for additional newsletters and articles we have written about how to handle the many challenges in executive job seeking.

Complimentary Offer for our Readers

To measure how your job search results compare to our recommended benchmarks, go to <u>www.optimarketllc.com/critique</u> and complete our brief Job Search Critique survey.

Notes

Notes

Notes